Marianne Faithfull:
The Ballad of a Homeless Queen

Newbury Publishing, LLC.

Copyright © 2023 **Newbury Publishing, LLC.**

All rights reserved. Except as permitted under the U.S. Copyright Act of 1976, no part of this publication may be reproduced, distributed, or transmitted in any form or by any means, or stored in a database or retrieval system, without the prior written permission of the publisher.

If you would like to use material from the book (other than for review purposes), prior written permission must be obtained by contacting the publisher at permission@newburypub.com
Thank you for your support of the author's rights.

Newbury Publishing, LLC
867 Boylston Street, 5th Floor, PMB 203, Boston, MA 02116

Visit our website at www.newburypub.com

The publisher is not responsible for websites (or their content) that are not owned by the publisher.

Cover and book design by Newbury Publishing, LLC.

The Newbury Publishing name and logo are trademarks of Newbury Publishing, LLC. All rights reserved.

First eBook Edition September 2023

CONTENTS

Chapter One 1

    Introduction

Chapter Two 7

    Marianne's Formative Years

Chapter Three 13

    Reduced Circumstances

Chapter Four 19

    Escape To London

Chapter Five 25

    Discovered

Chapter Six 29

    Marriage, Motherhood, And Mick

Chapter Seven 33

    Mick Jagger

Chapter Eight 37

    Mick's Muse

Chapter Nine 43

    Miss X

Chapter Ten 49

    Something Better

Chapter Eleven 53

    27 Club

Chapter Twelve 61

    Alone

CHAPTER ONE
Introduction

Marianne Faithfull is a Baby Boomer, a post war child and an icon of the Swinging Sixties. Her first career, which is chronicled in this book, was brief but multi-faceted. During this decade, this little bird was light and fragile.

Although she claims that she was not coerced or manipulated into the events that shaped her life, many of the forces that influenced her decision making existed long before she was born, some of them way back in time.

Her early childhood was winsome and steeped in romance. Her father was a scholar who studied and taught Roman literature and the Romance poets. In her formative years, he fostered in Marianne a love of reading that never left her. And as a quintessential English maiden, Medieval folk lore and songs coursed through her veins.

Major Glynn Faithfull's linguistic ability was his passport to a wartime life of international espionage and intrigue. He met and fell in love with his future wife, Marianne's mother, while on one of his assignments.

Eva's family drama played out in the cauldron of pre- and post-war Europe. Her aristocratic lineage and Jewish heritage were twin dangers on the war torn continent.

The gaiety of the Roaring Twenties, followed rapidly by the grim reality of the Great Depression and the suspense of the Second World War, had a profound effect on Eva and her family. Relief came when she was rescued by her husband-to-be.

Postwar England, even with its rations and social upheaval, was a haven for the immigrant and their beautiful and talented only child. The 1950s brought the twin constraints of conformity and 'reduced circumstances' for mother and daughter, so cruel in an age of prosperity. Survival once again became a necessary skill.

Marianne's mother took charge of her pre-teen and adolescent development, while nuns at the nearby convent were simultaneously responsible for her education and spiritual well being. Eva's nostalgic reminiscences of stardom and glamour contrasted sharply with the austere disciplines, of piety and chastity, required by the sisters of mercy.

The Swinging Sixties were manic. Everything was up for debate. Fashion, art and music changed constantly. The youth revolted and threw off the mantle of morality and materialism that their parents had fought long and hard to obtain.

Marianne's mission was to be a part of this revolution and she made plans to escape small town life and head for The City. Her first stop was Cambridge where a beau introduced her to the collective writings and lifestyles of the rebellious Beat Poets, and the lyrics of the thought provoking American songwriter Dylan. Her new love also smoked pot.

After a few gigs in coffee bars and a brief introduction to London's social life, she was catapulted into the centre of the celebrity scene. Her anonymity was lost as she became instantly recognisable as one of the IT girls.

Marianne mixed with a heady set of the most popular musicians of the day, all on the verge of stratospheric stardom. She counted among her friends, and lovers, members of famous bands such as the Beatles, the Rolling Stones and the Who. She had a brief brush with matrimony and motherhood, and a longer, very public, liaison with Mick Jagger.

Digging deep into her treasure trove of childhood stories, she equated her renowned love affair with the Rolling Stones lead man to the ancient Greek legend of Orpheus and Eurydice. The hero did everything mortally possible to save the maiden but broke the cardinal rule, and tragically lost his muse.

Her image and her ability, sadly, were not matched by the necessary emotional resilience needed for life in the fast lane. After a well documented, but ill-fated folk rock career, she crashed and slowly burned.

 Left to her own devices, she replaced the songs of the sirens with the more addictive and potentially fatal, psychedelic, hallucinogenic and narcotic drugs of her era. Her quest for ecstasy became a desperate need for an escape into oblivion, through the Doors of Perception, she thought she knew and understood.

From being 'very young, very beautiful, and very rich', she lost everything, for a long time. She was broke, sleeping in a bombed out relic of the war, living from day to day off massive doses of government issue heroin.

On the street, she experienced a kindness and care that she recognised and cherished, even through her drug induced haze. The darling of stage, screen and song was nurtured and protected by strangers. She embraced the obscurity and disappeared from the public eye for more than two years, until friends began to entice her back.

Perhaps John D. Loudermilk's lyrics of 'This Little Bird', one of the greatest songs from Marianne's early career, convey best the prescient pathos of this fragile young girl's experience of the Sixties.

There's a little bird that somebody sends
Down to the earth to live on the wind.
Borne on the wind and he sleeps on the wind
This little bird that somebody sends.

He's light and fragile and feathered sky blue,
So thin and graceful the sun shines through.
This little bird who lives on the wind,
This little bird that somebody sends.

He flies so high up in the sky
Out of reach of human eye.
And the only time that he touches the ground
Is when that little bird
Is when that little bird
Is when that little bird dies.

Marianne was too young to be a member of the 27 Club of musicians that the world of music has lost, but she was touched by all of them and so very nearly became a statistic of the era. Fortunately, she survived, took charge of her life and gave the world another five decades of her unique, avant garde talent.

In her career which began in 1964, she has produced more than twenty solo albums. Her most popular, according to the Billboard Top 100, were the first two, recorded in the 1960s. 'Marianne Faithfull' and 'Come My Way' reached number 15 and 12 respectively, on the UK charts.

There was a hiatus between 1967 and 1979, when Marianne wrote and recorded a number of songs on the album, 'Broken English'. The album was commercially successful and received critical acclaim. It went Gold in France and Platinum in Australia and Canada. Her follow up album two years later was Dangerous Acquaintances, which achieved Gold in those three countries.

She also recorded three live albums and nine compilations, and since 1981 has contributed to a further twenty albums, including one with Metallica. Her portfolio is eclectic.

Also in the 1960s, she had four hit singles in the Top 10. Her debut single, 'As Tears Go By', reached number 9; Come and Stay With Me (#4); This Little Bird (#6) and Summer Nights reached number 10. To date, Marianne has released 27 singles.

Her next chart topper was a cover version of Dr Hook and the Medicine Show's 'The Ballad of Lucy Jordan', in 1979. Her voice was far huskier, due to a severe bout of pharyngitis and years of smoking. She brought the emotion of a lifetime to the rendition. She was 33 years old.

Despite a recent health scare, Marianne still records songs, has a busy performance schedule and appears live at venues around the globe. She has an active social media presence and her work can be found on several streaming platforms where there have been millions of downloads.

CHAPTER TWO
Marianne's Formative Years

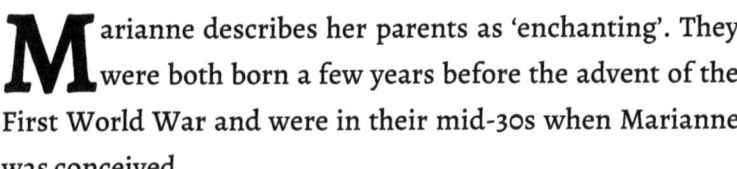

Marianne describes her parents as 'enchanting'. They were both born a few years before the advent of the First World War and were in their mid-30s when Marianne was conceived.

Her father, Glynn Faithfull, was born in England, of the upper classes, and went on to study literature. He could speak several languages and switched seamlessly between them, without any trace of an accent.

This made him useful to the British and allied forces during the period leading up to World War Two. He was recruited by MI6, the United Kingdom's secret intelligence services, and worked behind enemy lines. There he communicated fluently without being detected as either a foreigner or a spy. During his military career he rose to the rank of Major.

In the course of his espionage, he came to know members of the resistance and other anti-Nazi activists. Among these were Marianne's mother's family. Eva's father was Artur Wolfgang, Ritter von Sacher-Masoch, an Austrian knight, nobleman and renowned author. Her mother, Flora, was a Jewess who had converted to Catholicisim.

Eva Hermine was born in Budapest in 1912 while all was still well in that part of the former Austro-Hungarian Empire. She spent her early childhood on the family estates in Transylvania, which is now part of Romania. The family moved to the city of Vienna after World War One. This transition was echoed later in Marianne's life, and at a similar age.

Meanwhile in Germany, after the defeat and abdication of Kaiser Wilhelm, the Weimar Republic was established, by decree. Elections were held, resulting in the Republic being run by a loose coalition of representatives from a number of diverse parties.

In the early 1920s, the victors of the war demanded harsh financial reparations and the redistribution of large tracts of industrial land to neighbouring countries. This led to a period of crippling hyperinflation and intense austerity in Germany. The citizens of the country turned on the leaders of the Weimar Republic, holding them responsible for their plight. They were considered to be traitors and a cause of great tension in the country.

During this time, in neighbouring Austria, Eva attended a Catholic school and trained as a ballerina in the afternoons. Her coming of age, in the latter half of the 1920s, coincided with a period of surprising posterity in Germany and she moved to Berlin. The Roaring Twenties in the city was characterised by a decadence that people often express when they have been relieved of a great burden.

Eva worked as a performer, touring with the Max Reinhardt company, and dancing in nightclubs. She appeared in productions by Bertolt Brecht and Kurt Weill, whose work was later to become a great influence in Marianne's life. The bawdy lifestyle was portrayed in the 1972 film, 'Cabaret', which starred Liza Minnelli.

Reinhardt was a film and theatre producer who ran eleven theatres in Berlin, and a few more in Austria. While in his employ, Eva became increasingly exposed to radical, left wing theatre politics.

The party lasted until the repercussions of the 1929 Stock Exchange crash translated into the global financial crisis known as the Great Depression. This prolonged period of yet more financial hardship, caused the electorate of Germany to evict the unpopular Weimar Weimar regime. Adolf Hitler and his Third Reich took its place.

Kurt Weill's work was labeled as degenerate by the Nazis and he fled the country in 1933. Max Reinhardt, a Jew, took longer to accurately assess the growing negative sentiment towards his people. He fled Germany, for the United Kingdom, in 1938. Eva returned to her family home in Vienna, in the same year. Her security was short-lived, however, as Austria was annexed by the Nazis in 1939.

It was only Eva's father's impeccable Aryan ancestry and service to Germany during World War One that saved his Jewish wife from being sent to the ghettos and concentration camps. Their daughter was officially designated a Mischling, or mongrel.

Despite their precarious position, the family stored pamphlets for the resistance groups. Artur was later captured and tortured in order to reveal sensitive information. Thanks to his military training, his will was not broken and he refused to divulge any of his secrets.

His wife and daughter survived the war and liberation came at last. Tragically, in the exuberance of victory, soldiers of the Red Army raped an estimated one hundred thousand women, among them Flora and Eva. This trauma left both women with a lasting distaste for men, in general, and sex, in particular.

Major Faithfull was among the British contingent that arrived to liberate the occupied city. He met Eva when he came to inform the family that her brother was still alive. He stayed long enough to save her from further physical and psychological damage. The couple fell in love, and made plans to marry and settle in England.

As befitted her status as Baroness, Glynn took Eva to live in a castle on his 55 acre country estate in Oxfordshire. Marianne, their only child was born at Braziers Park, at the close of 1946, on 29 December.

Marianne loved growing up on the estate, which had historic links to several naval officers and parliamentary dignitaries. She learned to ride horses and enjoyed the sense of freedom she experienced in the open countryside. The building is a pseudo Gothic structure, built in the 17th century. There were many rooms for the young Marianne to explore.

She adored her father and followed in his footsteps, both literally and figuratively. She read widely from a young age and spoke as he did, with an upper class accent. He was an idealist that wanted to change the world. He was also an atheist.

Glynn Faithfull was one of the founders of a residential college at Braziers Park. The institution was started with the aim of conducting 'integrative social research'. The 'friendly society of unlike minds' was part of an experiment in communal living, interpersonal communication and barter for work systems. It still operates as an intentional community.

Essentially, it was a commune, with a constant throughput of enthusiastic and diverse young people. This environment of collective living did not appeal to Eva. The couple found it increasingly difficult to live together and finally parted ways when Marianne was seven.

CHAPTER THREE
Reduced Circumstances

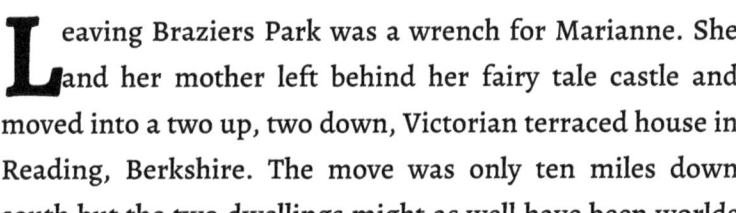

Leaving Braziers Park was a wrench for Marianne. She and her mother left behind her fairy tale castle and moved into a two up, two down, Victorian terraced house in Reading, Berkshire. The move was only ten miles down south but the two dwellings might as well have been worlds apart.

Reading lies at the confluence of the Thames and Kennet Rivers, about fifty miles due west of London. It was a large bustling and prosperous town in the 1950s, with aspirations of attaining city status. The area had escaped with little physical damage from the Blitz of the Second World War. Several lives had been lost however, which left emotional scars and united the community. In suburbia, people took pride in their gardens and vied for the manure left by the horse drawn carts that delivered their daily bread and milk.

Eva Hermine Sacher-Masoch, or Baroness Erisso, as she preferred to be addressed, found work as a waitress at the popular Sally's Cafe on Friar Street, in the central business district, about a mile as the crow flies from their home in Milman Street.

Marianne lost contact with her beloved father, almost immediately. As a consequence, for most of her life, she felt the deep sense of yearning, as if for an unrequited love. The busy professor remarried a decade later and had a son when Marianne was 20 years old. Simon Faithfull is a celebrated visual artist, both at home and abroad.

In Reading, Marianne's world shrank overnight. She had lost her playground and the freedom it gave her, and had difficulty adapting to their reduced circumstances. The uniformity of the houses and the working class conformity of the inhabitants stifled her, after the diversity and freedom of expression she had known at Braziers Park. She spoke and thought differently, and felt claustrophobic in the cramped quarters and crowded community.

Eva had attended a Catholic school in Vienna and wanted the same education for her child so she enrolled her in St Joseph's Roman Catholic Convent School in Reading.

Marianne excelled academically at the all girls school and grew up to be a beautiful young girl with natural blonde hair and a noteworthy figure. She loved singing from an early age and had hopes of becoming an opera singer. She took singing lessons and her tremulous soprano voice was well suited to the folk songs of old, which she and her friends sang on their picnic outings down by the river.

Her schooling was subsidised by means of a bursary. Whether this was due to her scholarly achievements, or her family's strained finances, is unknown. Despite being less than a mile from home, and two miles from her mother's place of work, Marianne became a weekly boarder at the school.

Whereas her father had adored her, the nuns only chastised her. They foresaw only trouble for this young lady who had both beauty and brains. Despite evidence to the contrary, they were convinced that she was a Scarlet Woman, destined to be all bad. No matter how hard she tried she could not shift their prejudice. Not even her conversion to Catholicism changed their thinking. Her frustration turned to rebellion.

At home, on the weekends, she received a different message from her mother. Eva was convinced that as soon as Marianne moved to London, she would be 'discovered'.

Eva filled the house with music from her days as a dancer in Berlin, working for Max Reinhardt and performing in Kurt Weill productions. She regaled Marianne with her stories of her stint in the spotlight, and her life on the road, touring.

One of the great social changes in 1950s Britain was the mass production of television sets. Like the Model T Ford, it became almost ubiquitous in suburban households. When Queen Elizabeth was crowned in 1953, there were still few sets per neighbourhood and people gathered in groups at friends' houses to watch it.

The event sparked a national explosion of optimism and prosperity, which brought with it a wave of consumer spending. Soon families were gathering in their own homes to watch the box.

At first, the only channel was BBC with its fairly staid, adult-centred content which sought constantly to inform, rather than entertain. The Postmaster General limited broadcast hours, and no programming was allowed between 6 and 7 pm. This hiatus was known as "toddlers' truce", and was intended to fool the children in the household into thinking that the station had shut down for the night.

In 1955, a new channel was opened. The general population found ITV much more enjoyable and the sale of television sets soared. Game shows, comedies and soap operas kept people glued to their sets.

Programmes were imported from America and this is how the British started to absorb the culture from across the pond. Elvis was the king of pop in the late 1950s, and teenagers went crazy for his gyrating dance moves. Rock and roll artists mesmorised new audiences and working class youth across Britain were inspired to produce their own music. Cities like Birmingham, Liverpool and London exploded with new talent.

This audiovisual input was music to Marianne's ears, and she yearned to escape from suburbia to the bright city lights. At the age of 16 she started making concrete plans to do just that.

CHAPTER FOUR
Escape to London

When Marianne was in her mid teens she was every boy's dream date. In February 1963, one hopeful suitor asked her to a Valentine's Day Ball at Cambridge University. Presumably he was a student there because very little is known about him after this invitation.

For this is where Marianne met and fell in love with John Dunbar, a hip young boy with long hair and small round glasses similar to those later made famous by John Lennon of the Beatles. She forgot about her date and spent the evening in the exclusive company of her new conquest.

Marianne and John, like many young lovers, became inseparable. It must have been a frustrating time for them because Cambridge was 90 miles away from Reading and 60 miles due north of London.

John introduced Marianne to the music of Bob Dylan and the writings and poetry of the Beat Generation. There is video evidence of her and Joan Baez singing As Tears Go By in Dylan's hotel room while he types. She found out later that he was infatuated with her and was typing a poem to her. She turned him down and he tore up the poem. They are still friends.

She became familiar with names such as Allen Ginsberg, William S Burroughs and Jack Kerouac. She met many of them and Ginsberg and Burroughs were present at separate pivotal points in her life. Their thinking reminded her of the intellectual environment she had been exposed to at Braziers Park.

Much like the 21st century is defined by the thoughts, attitudes and behaviour of Generations X, Y, Z and Alpha, the 20th century was equally influenced by members of consecutive generations.

The Beat Generation was a subset of its time. This Bohemian group of alternative thinkers were born in the first quarter of the 20th century, in the era assigned to the Great Generation. They were her father's contemporaries, except that he was British and they were American. They were old enough to understand the hardships of the Great Depression and the males were almost all eligible for conscription during the Second World War.

These authors and poets succeeded famous American authors, of the Lost Generation, such as Ernest Hemingway, F.Scott Fitzgerald and William Faulkner. Many of these literary giants lived and worked in postwar Paris where there were more women than men, the food was great and accommodation was cheap, especially when it was paid for in dollars.

The term Lost Generation was coined by Gertrude Stein, because she viewed them as wandering around the city aimlessly, trying to make sense of their world through an alcohol-soaked haze. They wrote mostly about vacuous characters who specialised in decadence, corruption and frivolity. The Great Gatsby and The Sun Also Rises are novels typical of the era.

The Beat Generation rejected this materialistic narrative, explored Eastern and other religions and experimented with drugs. While they fueled and ignited their creativity with alcohol and marijuana, their followers from the next, 'silent' generation, moved on to hallucinogenic and psychedelic drugs, such as LSD. They were promiscuous, anti-establishment vagabonds with few permanent ties.

John Dunbar was a wartime baby, born on the cusp of the Silent Generation and the Baby Boomers. He was a British national who was born in Mexico City, in 1943, and spent his early childhood in Moscow. His father was a film maker and the cultural attaché to post war Russia.

At the time he and Marianne met, he was 20 and she was 17. She was independent and unsupervised. He was an art student, and was soon to become a film maker and art dealer. He smoked pot and was one of the early partakers of LSD. Much later in life he held a symposium on LSD and its effect on the visual arts.

Through his art dealings, he met up and coming musicians who had been advised to invest in artwork. Among these were members of the Beatles and the Rolling Stones and their management. He was invited to several of their parties, and became a regular feature of the Swinging Sixties scene in London.

Far from being a global phenomenon, as its reputation would suggest, the Swinging Sixties was a British phenomenon, with the focus on London, and more specifically, the West End. It was a cultural revolution driven by middle class Baby Boomers, in the middle years of the decade. Postwar London was changed from a drab, dreary monochrome to a vibrant, Instagram-worthy, psychedelic hub of all forms of art.

Trends were set daily in the fashion, music and arts industries. The Union Jack became the symbol of the British Invasion. It appeared on commodities of all shapes and sizes, including dresses, home decor and cars, such as the Mini.

Mary Quant made the mini skirt and Carnaby Street household names. Models were skinny with names like Twiggy. Their hair was long and their skirts short. Wide eyes sparkled in the flawless faces of the English roses.

It was the after effect and cause of an economic boom. Everything was new and modern and transitory. Some of the sentiment was underpinned by a nihilistic fatalism that was fuelled by the constant fear of nuclear war. Drugs gave the illusion that the party could last forever.

Conscription had been abolished so young men, with disposable income, were at a loose end. Sex was freely available, especially since the legal distribution of birth control pills began in 1960.

The undisputed royalty were the pop stars and rock musicians. The 'London Sound' included the Rolling Stones, the Who, the Kinks and the Small Faces. The Beatles, who hailed from Liverpool, were honorary members. Female singers included Dusty Springfield, Lulu, Cilla Black and Sandie Shaw, none of whom were locals.

This was the milieu into which Marianne had been trying, unsuccessfully, to launch her singing career by looking for gigs at restaurants and coffee shops. Secretly though, she harboured notions of marrying John and settling down to become a scholar's wife. The thought of dinner parties with the intelligentsia, with long discussions about the arts, that stretched long into the night, appealed to her.

It was at a party, to launch the Rolling Stones, when Marianne first went up to London, that she was discovered, just as her mother had said she would be.

CHAPTER FIVE
Discovered

People at the party described Marianne's entrance as 'a moment when the music was turned down'. Her beauty caught the attention of everyone in the room when she arrived on John's arm.

One of the attendees was Andrew Oldham, the young manager of the Rolling Stones. Marianne describes how he made a beeline for John, and asked him if she could sing. Their conversation continued in front of her, as if she were not there. When John said he didn't know, Andrew claimed that it didn't matter.

Andrew Loog Oldham was a hustler from an early age. His American father had been shot down during the war, over the English Channel. He died in June of 1943, seven months before Andrew was born. Andrew's mother was an Australian, living in England. She chose to remain in the country and raised him in Oxfordshire. He spent his teenage years making money off French tourists.

When he was nineteen, he was introduced to the Rolling Stones and immediately saw an opportunity to develop their image as the bad boys of rock. He marketed them as the antithesis of the clean cut looks and seemingly conformist personae of their rivals, the wildly popular Beatles. Whereas the Beatles wore uniform suits and had their iconic 'Beatles' hairstyle, the Stones were encouraged to grow their hair long, wear leather and generally look scruffy.

The enmity between the Beatles and Rolling Stones was a construct developed by Andrew Oldham and strengthened by the media. Fans were incited to choose to follow either the Stones or the Beatles. There was no middle road.

In reality, the members of the bands were friends and collaborated on various songs and albums. The Beatles recommended the Stones to the record label Decca, and helped write the song 'I Wanna Be Your Man'. They guested on each other's tracks and their images appeared on the other band's album covers.

The Rolling Stones recorded over 90 albums, 120 singles, and a range of box sets, video albums and music videos. Until 1983, all seventeen albums that they released, were ranked in the Top 3. Their record sales are approaching a quarter of a billion.

Billboard magazine ranks them as the second Greatest Of All Time artists, behind their old rivals the Beatles. Richards, Mick Jagger and the two remaining Beatles are among the top eleven richest rock stars of all time.

Such was the calibre and power of the man who discovered Marianne. In her wide eyes and naivety, he saw a virginal young girl who would appeal to a broad audience. He offered her a contract without hesitation, which she accepted without parental guidance, thinking all the while of her mother's prophetic words. She went back home and immediately cut ties with the convent, without completing her A levels.

Back in London, Andrew Oldham instructed Mick Jagger and Keith Richards to lock themselves in a room somewhere and not to come out until they had a song that conjured up images of life behind the cloistered walls of a convent.

Keith Richards recalls that they humoured Oldham, but had no intention of fulfilling the brief. They figured they would emerge after a few hours, apologise profusely and get on with their partying. As luck would have it they were inspired, and in a matter of hours had successfully penned the future hit song, As Tears Go By.

Marianne was given little time to learn about studio recording, before the song was released late in 1964. The Rolling Stones also recorded it the following year. Both versions were chart toppers. Marianne's debut single reached the Billboard Top 10 in the United Kingdom and number 22, in the United States.

Much later in life, Marianne said that she felt that she was too young for the song. She had not earned the right or learned enough about life to sing the poignant words. She recorded it again when her voice was much raspier, and she was right.

The song endures and still forms part of the Rolling Stones line up on their concert tours. Mick Jagger and Taylor swift performed it together during the Stones' '50 and Counting' tour in 2013.

1965 was an eventful year for the John and Marianne. They discovered that she was pregnant and she and John married in May. Peter Asher of 'Peter and Gordon' fame was John's best man, and it is believed that Allen Ginsberg, one of the Beat poets, accompanied them on their honeymoon.

The couple moved to Knightsbridge, a fashionable upmarket district in the centre of London. They lived about a half a miles from Harrods, the world famous apartment store. Their address was 29 Lennox Gardens, one of the most exclusive garden squares in the area, and a far cry from Milman Road in Reading.

John and his business partner, Barry Miles opened the Indica Gallery in London, with the aim of exhibiting the work of cutting edge artists. The venture lasted for two years only, and John then spent his time producing his own art.

Their son Nicholas was born in November 1965. Marianne was still only 18 years old.

CHAPTER SIX
Marriage, Motherhood, and Mick

Marianne had difficulty juggling her various responsibilities. She was naive about what it required to be a wife and a mother of an infant, and had difficulty juxtaposing her life of glamour with the domesticity of running a household.

John was often away on business or with friends, leaving her alone with the baby. This did not stop her from running with the in crowd. Alcohol consumption, smoking and the odd puff of marijuana became the norm.

She suddenly had seemingly unlimited cash to spend but had no concept of accounting. John claims that she was, simultaneously overly concerned about money, and a shopaholic, buying expensive items that she did not need. Marianne attempted to hide them from him while he was out, but he invariably found them and arguments ensued.

Communication channels broke down further because Marianne did not deem it necessary to consult with John about her career decisions. Nor did she tell him about them once they had been made. He went away on one of his trips abroad and on his return discovered that As Tears Go By had entered the Top 10 on the music charts, and that Marianne was an overnight sensation.

Notwithstanding the confusion at home, she was brimming with confidence and having a wonderful time. She was young, beautiful, rich and rising fast. She recorded more songs, among them 'This Little Bird' and 'Come and Stay With Me'. She was living in two different worlds.

Andrew Oldham's nose was out of joint because the innocent image he had created for her did not suit the reality of her being, first pregnant, and then a wife and mother. He resented not having her available at his beck and call, and had no sympathy for her attempts to balance a career and home life.

John and Marianne eventually drifted apart as John found it increasingly difficult to relate to Marianne and started spending more and more time with his own pursuits. She decided that marriage was not for her and she and John separated. They finalised their divorce in 1970.

Marianne left her husband when her son was a year old. She and Nicholas had no fixed abode and squatted with a succession of long suffering friends, including Brian Jones, one of the founding members of the Rolling Stones, and

Anita Pallenberg, who were a couple at the time. She started smoking steadily and actively experimented with LSD.

A friend recalls how she came home to find water gushing down the steps from the bathroom above. Marianne was in the bath, fascinated by how the soap was lathering on her skin, totally oblivious to the damage that was being caused as the house flooded.

Her career had taken off and she was recording in two genres, namely folk rock and pop music. Andrew Oldman decided that she needed a sexier image and chose more risqué outfits for her publicity shots. He arranged a photo shoot and had her dress in black lingerie.

Marianne became the poster girl of the British Invasion. This was a cultural phenomenon that reversed the trend of importing US music to the United Kingdom. Until the early 1960s, British artists had had difficulty breaking into the US market. Only Cliff Richards had managed a Top 40 hit there.

In the mid 60s, a number of British bands and solo artists visited the United States and appeared on television. Beatlemania kickstarted the invasion. Other bands that toured included the Rolling Stones, the Hollies, Herman's Hermits and the Who. Tom Jones, the Welsh sex symbol, and female artists such as Cilla Black and Petula Clark, also made inroads.

Videos of Marianne's songs appeared on television. She was dressed in demure outfits that were far more suitable for family audiences. With her pretty face and thick blonde hair she was responsible for making a generation of young boys fall headlong in love with her. Many of these passions endure to this day.

But already the strain on her voice from substance abuse was evident, and her unblinking stare into the camera while she mouthed the words speaks of a dullness that was new.

She could often be found in the company of the Rolling Stones and claims to have slept with Mick Jagger, Keith Richards and Brian Jones. Without a covert seductive strategy, she managed to appear hard to get. This intrigued Mick Jagger who had his pick of men and women fawning all over him. Jerry Hall, who was later to become his wife, called him a dangerous, serial sexual predator.

Marianne recalls that her behaviour and attitude towards Mick Jagger stemmed from the feelings of abandonment and unrequited love that she felt in her relationship with her father. In the back of her mind were also her mother's musings about men. Marianne often had to get drunk or high to still these voices before making love to anyone.

Marianne ignored Jagger for months before they finally paired up. He was dating Chrissie Shrimpton at the time. Her older sister, Jean Shrimpton, was a 1960s icon and reputed to be the first super model. On the night it happened, Marianne just happened to stay longer than all the others did, until they were alone together.

CHAPTER SEVEN
Mick Jagger

By the time Mick Jagger and Marianne Faithfull became an item in 1966, he had the reputation of being the bad boy of Rock and Roll. Andrew Oldham played on Mick's sexual ambiguity and cast him as an anti-establishment, androgynous delinquent.

Oldham's attitude was that no publicity was bad publicity. The Rolling Stones got into a number of scrapes during their early career. During one live performance in Blackpool, Keith Richards became annoyed with members of the audience spitting onto the stage, so he kicked one of the patrons in the head.

In Berlin, Mick Jagger goose stepped across the stage and raised a salute similar to those used in Nazi Germany. Instead of invoking a negative reaction, many in the audience stood to attention and saluted back. A fight broke out which spilled into the street and became a riot. The incident led to the banning of live Rock and Roll performances in the city for twenty-five years.

Although his energy was electric and he clearly had charisma, Mick's background was somewhat tame. Michael Phillip Jagger was born during the war, in the summer of 1943. The family lived in Dartford, Kent in the south east corner of England.

His mother was an Australian born hairdresser and a proficient housewife, while his father and grandfather were both teachers. His father specialised in physical education and helped popularise basketball as a sport in England.

Mick was lithe and athletic, and excelled at basketball and cross country running. He and his father shared an interest in rock climbing, and appeared on television together when Mick was a teenager.

His parents were upwardly mobile and could afford to send him to the best grammar school in their area. None of his teachers can recall a rebellious streak or having had any trouble with him. The consensus among his classmates was that he did not stand out in the crowd. At home he led a quiet, disciplined life.

Mick loved to sing but his music taste differed from that of his peers. While they preferred the juke box music of Buddy Holly, Patsy Cline and the Everly Brothers, he listened to the AFM – the American Forces Network, and became enamoured with rhythm and blues icons, such as Chuck Berry and Bo Diddley.

He and a few friends formed a flegling band called Little Boy Blue and the Blue Boys. Mick had a different persona behind the microphone. His favourite song was La Bamaba. While he sang it, he preened and pranced, much to the amusement of his friends and family.

When he left school, he enrolled at the London School of Economics in order to study finance. He was a diligent and unassuming scholar who enjoyed his course work and achieved good grades. One fateful day, while on his way back home from college, Mick bumped into Keith Richards, an old friend and neighbour from his primary school days.

Rumour has it that Keith was carrying his guitar and Mick was carrying a pile of R & B albums. This sparked off a conversation about music, and they discovered that they shared similar interests.

Keith was a few months younger than Mick. They had been neighbours and attended the same primary school up until the time that Mick's family moved to a more affluent area. Keith had grown up in a working class family, with roots in local politics. His grandfather had toured in a jazz band and had given Keith his first guitar and music lessons. Keith was studying art when he met up with Mick again in 1961.

The two began frequenting the Ealing Jazz Club in the western suburbs of London to listen to R&B. There they met Brian Jones, who was already an established musician and was looking to put a band together. The three began jamming together and eventually moved into a London flat together.

Jagger, Richards and Jones played at venues for free and were generally well received. However, with Jones and Richards on guitar, and Jagger on vocals, their style was eclectic and ill-defined. The three leads needed a rhythm section. It was not until Bill Wyman joined them on bass guitar, and Charlie Watts on drums, that the band gelled.

Initially they played a mix of R& B and early rock and roll covers. Andrew Oldman astutely assessed the pop scene and determined that the band would not endure unless they wrote and performed some of their own songs. Jagger and Richards followed in the footsteps of Lennon and McCartney of the Beatles and became the band's songwriters.

It was at the band's launch in 1964, that Marianne Faithfull and the Rolling Stones' worlds collided. The Jagger / Richards duo were asked to write a debut song for her. They wrote As Tears Go By which became a hit for her, and for them, when they recorded it the following year.

CHAPTER EIGHT
Mick's Muse

Marianne was funny, charming and an aristocrat. She may not have been educated beyond her O levels but she was intelligent, well read and spoke with a posh accent. She had an ethereal aura of mystery and adventure about her.

Marianne became Mick's muse. She influenced his fashion sense and introduced him to a wider world of literature, recommending what books he should read. They had long conversations that stretched well into the night. She also introduced him to an upper class social circle, something that middle class Mick aspired to.

They collaborated on songs and enjoyed an active social life together, including several trips to exotic destinations abroad. Miarianne and Mick were in love, and fêted as the golden couple of Rock and Roll. They lived together in a grand house in Chelsea, one of London's upmarket boroughs.

In reality, she found it to be a misogynistic environment where women were not expected to express their opinions. She was a bright and articulate young woman but found that she had to remain silent when the men were in discussion.

When the band got together, the wives and girlfriends were excluded and ignored. They would go on shopping expeditions to spend their partners' money on the latest fashions, and to test the latest designer drugs. They were Sloane Rangers before the term was coined.

Marianne's dependence on recreational drugs and alcohol grew. She used them to fill the hollowness she felt inside.

She left her singing career as she felt there was not enough room for two careers in their relationship. She turned to stage and film and tried her hand at acting.

She had a small part in the film, "I'll never forget What's 'is Name", starring Oliver Reed and Orson Welles. She starred as a young ill-fated temptress dressed in black leather, in the French film, 'La Motocyclette', the Girl on the Motorcycle. She also sang in German on a French television comedy.

In the theatre, she first played one of the sisters, opposite Glanda Jackson, in the Checkhov play, 'Three Sisters'. Later, in 1969, she played Ophelia, in Shakespeare's Hamlet. It was her habit to get high during the intervals which leant credibility to the madness required of the role in subsequent scenes.

Mick, despite his showmanship and rebellious image, always managed to maintain a measure of control over his use of substances. Marianne, on the other hand, was enamoured with hallucinogenic drugs and even waxed lyrical about LSD, live on television.

In one famous interview she seemed to be justifying the existence of the drug and promoting its consumption, as she tried to explain to her host how drugs were the Doors of Perception into an alternative reality.

This thinking was based on Aldous Huxley's book by the same name. One of his quotes is as follows, "When the doors of perception are cleansed, men will see things as they truly are, infinite." Jim Morrison was inspired by this book to call his band The Doors.

Marianne became a poster child for a growing movement known as 'Psychedelia'. It started with the Beat poets who smoked cannabis and popped Benzedrines, and then wrote about it. At the same time, the official channels were experimenting with an hallucinogenic drug known as LSD. This drug made its way underground and became known as 'acid'. As drugs go, it was not particularly addictive but it did create a desire in some users to experiment further.

Marianne moved on to cocaine and later heroin. She began to be an embarrassment at social functions. There is a well reported incident at the Earl of Warwick's castle, where a lavish dinner had been arranged in the honour of the golden couple. That night Marianne was popping Mandrax downers and fell asleep, with her face in the soup.

It was a disaster for the social climbing Rolling Stone, and after this incident, Mick frequently went to functions without her. She was an out of control wild child who had become a liability.

Mick's drug of choice was sex. Ostensibly, he and Marianne were in a monogamous relationship, but in reality, he was a serial womaniser. And Marianne retaliated from time to time with her own liaisons. One particular pentagon of entanglements became well known.

Keith Richards had wooed Anita Pallenberg away from Brian Jones. While Mick Jagger and Anita were working together on a film project, they slept together. In retaliation, Keith Richards and Marianne had a brief fling, before they each went back to their respective partners. Perhaps the ultimate revenge was that Marianne commented that the sex with Keith was 'memorable', something she did not attribute to Mick Jagger.

During the band's wild days, Bill Wyman was the champion stud in the group, sleeping with the most number of women, by far. He was followed by Brian Jones, with Mick Jagger featuring in the mid range. Keith Richards slept with very few of the women available and Charlie Watts remained faithful to his wife throughout.

Another of Mick's publicised relationship while he was with Marianne, was with Marsha Hunt. She is reported to have had his first child but spent a decade trying to get him to acknowledge responsibility.

CHAPTER NINE
Miss X

A year into their relationship, Marianne's reputation was tarnished by the media to such an extent that it took years for her to recover. She believes that the event that triggered this fall from grace was engineered.

The authorities were alarmed at the bald faced culture of drug taking amongst the rock and roll elite, in clear contravention of the newly promulgated Dangerous Drugs Act of 1965. They wanted to put an end to it and needed a high profile incident to make their case. The news hounds, for their part, were rabid for sensational material, on the swinging celebrities, for their front pages.

In January of 1967, Mick Jagger was mistakenly identified by The News of the World as an attendee at a party, who brazenly boasted about his drugs and showed off his stash of hashish. It had, in fact, been Brian Jones that the reporter had overheard. Jagger had an alibi that negated the allegation, and consequently sued the tabloid newspaper for libel.

The newspaper realised its error and redoubled its efforts to portray Jagger in a negative light. Reporters began stalking the members of the band to support their case. The stakes were high for Jagger and the group because criminal convictions could lead to the visas they needed, to tour the United States, being denied.

Early in February 1967, Marianne, Mick Jagger, Keith Richards and a few friends had planned a fun weekend at Redlands, Keith's newly acquired country retreat. The plan was to introduce Mick to acid. George Harrison and his girlfriend had been invited but left after dinner.

Brian Jones had yet to arrive when the raid occurred, and was told not to bother coming. Andrew Oldham was at the party but bolted and fled to the United States for several months. Friends said they had never seen him pack his suitcase so fast. It was not long after that the Rolling Stones' Svengali decided that he had had enough of the monster that he had created, and he and the band parted ways.

There were several other guests present, including William Burroughs, one of the original Beat poets. Burroughs was much older than the rest of the group, having been born in 1914. He had already had his fair share of run-ins with the authorities. In 1951, he accidentally shot and killed his wife while under the influence.

Marianne was the only female on the premises at the time of the bust. She had already partaken of the drugs and decided to take a bath. Half way through her ablutions, eighteen members of the local constabulary, including two female officers, arrived in seven police cars and stormed the premises,.

Marianne was naked when the action began. On leaving the bathroom, the only covering she could find was a large fur throw on one of the beds. Thus when she was found by the policewomen, she was essentially nude, except for the throw.

This could be considered to be prescribed behaviour for Marianne. Her grand-uncle on her mother's side, Leopold von Sacher-Masoch, who was an author of erotica, had written a novel, entitled 'Venus in Fur'. As a result of the novel, the word 'masochism' was coined

The remains of a few joints of marijuana, some amphetamine pills and a small quantity of heroin were found. Richards was charged because the party was held on his premises, while Jagger gallantly stated that the pills were his, whereas they were Marianne's.

A trial and much publicity ensued. Jagger and Richards had an opportunity to dress up for the press and portray themselves as romantic heroes. They were both sentenced to jail time but through the intervention of a conservative newspaper they were freed after only one night.

Many believe this was a publicity stunt orchestrated by Andrew Oldham while still in self-imposed exile abroad. The incident only served to enhance the carefully crafted bad boy image of the band.

But, as one journalist wrote, 'notoriety had a way of sliding off the boys and sticking on Faithfull'. Another wrote, "If you couldn't go after the Beatles, you went after the Rolling Stones. If you couldn't go after the Stones, you went after Marianne." The rules were different for men and women.

The first pop star drug raid had profound repercussions for Marianne. She was not named in newspaper articles but referred to as 'Miss X', or 'Naked Woman in Fur Rug'. Sordid fabrications were made about an orgy. With Marianne being the only woman present, this was an assault on her femininity and dignity.

She was portrayed as a loose woman, an unfit mother and a depraved drug soaked divorcee. In her own words, she was 'demeaned, diminished and trampled'. Her feminine self was besmirched.

The ongoing publicity from the bust and the subsequent trials and appeals profoundly affected Marianne's mother. She became depressed, turned to alcohol for solace, and eventually had to give up her job.

Richards and Jagger became paranoid and embarked on a witch hunt to discover who had alerted the police. They suspected, inter alia, Patrick their chauffeur, Schneiderman, the drug dealer on the day, and Nick Kramer, an associate of the band who was present at the party. Through third parties they had Patrick and Kramer beaten up. Schneiderman fled before they could track him down.

In 1967, after all these events had taken place, Marianne was still only twenty. She had grown up under public scrutiny. Much like her response to the nuns who labeled her as bad, she developed a rebellious attitude towards society as a whole. If everyone thought she was bad, she would do her best to live up to that image, and if necessary, exceed all expectations.

She accepted her new role and ramped up her drug intake. There were always pushers who lurked in the shadows of celebrities, waiting to explore every opportunity. She was soon hopelessly hooked.

She feels that Mick Jagger protected her from others, and to a large extent from the consequences of her own actions. It seems, however, that she lacked guidance from others.

Andrew Oldham saw an opportunity to explore her naivety and packaged her as a dichotomous angel cum nymphet. And her mother, who had filled her heads with thoughts of a nomadic show business lifestyle, was wooed by and enamoured with Mick Jagger. He had bought her a cottage in the countryside.

Marianne had several female British contemporaries who were perhaps not exposed to as much public scrutiny as she was. The press hounded her because of her association with the Rolling Stones, and were more interested in reporting on her moral failures than on her talent and success.

Petula Clark was fifteen years her senior, but Cilla Black, Lulu and Sandie Shaw were her contemporaries, and also debuted in 1964. They were all from working class backgrounds, far from the London limelight, with few advantages as teenagers. Cilla Black was raised in Liverpool and was a friend of the Beatles. They arranged for their manager Brian Epsteen to represent her professionally.

The Scottish born Lulu was discovered as a fifteen year old and was strictly managed throughout the formative years of her career. Sandie Shaw, from Dagenham in Essex, had a similar experience of being 'discovered', but perhaps far from the city lights, she did not succumb to the same temptations.

CHAPTER TEN
Something Better

In 1968, Marianne is credited for inspiring Mick to write the song, 'Sympathy for the Devil', after she gave him a copy of the book, 'The Master and the Margarita' by Russian author Mikhail Bulgakov. It had only recently been translated into English. The song led to further bad publicity and the Stones being labeled as Devil worshippers.

The two also collaborated on a song called, 'Sister Morphine', which Marianne sang first. The Stones later included their rendition in the album 'Sticky Fingers' Marianne co-wrote the song but was not credited when it was released. A long legal battle ensued.

The song is appeared on the b-side of Marianne's song, 'Something Better'. The lyrics tell the story of a dying man who is asking his nurse for more morphine to relieve him of his pain. The authorities viewed it differently and only 500 copies were sold in the United Kingdom before it was removed from the shelves.

By late 1968, Marianne's drug habit was spiralling out of control, and Mick was in between much publicised flings with Anita Pallenberg and Marsha Hunt.

Nevertheless, Marianne was in the advanced stages of pregnancy and the couple were excited about having their first child. They had chosen the name Corrina for their daughter. Sadly, Marianne lost the child in November of that year. She injured herself and terminated the baby when she fell off a chair.

Marianne went into a tailspin and once again turned to drugs for comfort. Mick appeared insensitive to her emotional turmoil and to some extent blamed her for the loss of their child. Despite his bohemian lifestyle, and his seemingly uncontrollable libido, he longed for the stable family life that he had enjoyed growing up in Kent. He later went on to father eight children from five women, four of them with Jerry Hall.

A few weeks later, in early December, Marianne appeared in the Rolling Stones, Rock and Roll Circus. This event was held in a circus tent, in an actual circus. Only those who were invited could attend.

It was a tedious affair that lasted thirteen hours, from 2 pm on 11 December to 5 am on 12 December. By the time the last act performed, everyone was exhausted. The line up included Jethro Tull, the Who, John Lennon and Yoko Ono, Marianne, and, of course, The Rolling Stones.

The event eventually did turn out to be a bit of a circus. Brian Jones was high and seemed incapable of performing. It was to be his last appearance with the group. Mick Jagger felt that the group's overall effort was sub par, and that they had been outplayed by the Who.

He refused to allow the BBC to air it, and an edited version of the video was only released in 1996. It was received with critical acclaim, possibly because of the youthful appearance of Jagger when he and the group had already moved on in years.

Marianne was recorded singing 'Something Better'. The lyrics were written by Gerald Goffin, an American lyricist, who was at one time married to Carole King. The instrumentals were pre-recorded while she sat.

She sat, almost motionless in the centre of the ring, while the camera panned around her. Her iconic purple dress is reminiscent of the outfits Andrew Oldham chose during her 'sex kitten' phase, and is remembered fondly by many. Her hair was cut short in a pixie style which framed her face beautifully.

However, her eyes and wry smiles betray the increasing despair she was experiencing. Her posh accent is noticeable but her husky voice hints at abuse. The little bird was trapped in a gilded cage.

He walks along singing his fairy song
Picking up magic that grows at his feet.

She says the same her peculiar way
Dreaming good fortune on everyone's street.
Say, hey, have you heard, blue whiskey's the rage,
I'll send you a jug in the morning.

It is absurd to live in a cage,
You know there's got to be something better.
As they go by, don't look with eagle's eyes
Smile on your jailers until they grow weak.
Nothing can compare to something that's almost there
To tear up the madness that all of us seek.

Say, hey, have you heard, blue whiskey's the rage,
I'll send you a jug in the morning.
It is absurd to live in a cage,
You know there's got to be something better.

CHAPTER ELEVEN
27 Club

1969 unfortunately was not a better year. Brain Jones, one of the founding members of the Rolling Stones, and one of Marianne's early conquests, was found dead at the bottom of the swimming pool at his country home. He was 27 years old.

Controversy still surrounds his death but the official ruling was one of accidental death or death by misadventure. He drowned while under the influence of alcohol and narcotics. His death occurred three weeks after his official break with the Rolling Stones, the band that he had founded.

Lewis Brian Hopkins Jones was a year older than his band members. He grew up in an affluent middle class family in Cheltenham in Gloucestershire, about 100 miles north east of London.

His father was an aeronautical engineer by day and a piano teacher after hours. His mother played the piano and the organ and sang in the church choir. Brian grew up hearing classical music in his home, and sang in the choir with his mom but preferred the Blues.

Brian was a talented all-rounder. He was bright scholar who never really applied himself at academics. He played the clarinet in the school orchestra, and enjoyed badminton and diving, despite his history of respiratory ailments which included croup and asthma.

His approach to life was ill-disciplined and nonconformist, and he often fell foul of the authorities. At the age of 17 he fathered his first child which was given up for adoption by his girlfriend's family. He fathered a further four children, from four different women, none of whom he raised.

He left school and home, in disgrace, and spent the summer busking around northern Europe. Eventually, he exhausted his cash and the charity of strangers and had to return to England. He applied for a scholarship to study art at the Cheltenham Art College but was refused when one of his referees called him an irresponsible drifter.

He moved to London and started working at the Ealing Club. While there, he advertised for musicians to join a band and that is how he met Jagger and Richards. He named the group Rolling Stones after the Muddy Waters song, "Rollin' Stone". The group met their Blues idol in 1964, while on tour in Chicago, and were greatly encouraged by him.

Brian's role in the Rolling Stones was as a multi instrumentalist. He played the slide guitar, as well as electric and acoustic guitars, the sitar and the harmonica. He and Keith Richards played the lead and rhythm sections interchangeably. He can also be heard as the backing vocals on some tracks.

Whereas Mick and Keith had been caught with controlled substances on several occasions, they had been spooked into abstaining by these run ins with the authorities, and reined in their substance abuse.

Brian was less fortunate. He accumulated a string of offences and was finally lumbered with a criminal record. This meant that he would not be granted a visa to travel to the United States, a move that was seen as crucial to the Rolling Stone's global success.

Tensions also grew over leadership of the band. Andrew Oldham had correctly foreseen that the band needed to write their own original material. Mick Jagger and Keith Richards followed the examples of other songwriters such as the Beatles, and had become a successful songwriting team, and Mick Jagger was clearly the front man of the band. Andrew Oldham and the other members of the band, increasingly marginalised Brian.

His drug addiction caused him to miss appointments and to deliver lacklustre performances when he did appear. One telling incident occurred when the other band members recorded Red Rooster in the studio without inviting him. They left clear instructions on his guitar where he was to add his contribution. Brian completed the song alone.

His love life can best be described as erratic. This changed when he met Anita Pallenberg, an ex-model. They stayed together for two years but it was a violent and volatile relationship characterised by destructive cycle of drug dependence, as well as physical and emotional abuse. Brian is reported to have broken his hand on Anita's face, but she delivered as good as she got.

After yet another spate of binging and drug busts, Keith, Brian and Anita decided to leave town until the situation cooled down. They were headed across France to Morocco when Brian became ill and had to be hospitalised. The other two carried on without him, and according to Keith it took only about five hours in the back of the car for them to bond. When they returned, Brian was no longer part of the equation.

He became increasingly morose, uncooperative and self-absorbed. Eventually, the rest of the group drove to his country home to confronted him and tell him that he was no longer welcome to be part of the group. He retreated to his home to lick his wounds.

Brian was in the process of arranging renovations to the property when he died. There was speculation at the time that he had become embroiled in a dispute with a contractor over payment. The individual involved was cleared of all suspicion.

Before the tragedy, the Rolling Stones had organised a free concert to be held in Hyde Park, London, on 5 July, two days after Brian's death. The group had not performed live for two years, and the Stones in the Park concert was intended to be an introduction to their new guitarist, Mick Taylor.

There was speculation that the event would be cancelled but the group decided to hold it instead as a memorial to Brian. A quarter of a million people turned up to pay tribute. Unlike previous Rolling Stones live events, the crowd was orderly and respectful and left quietly. There were no incidents.

None of the band members had the stomach to make the arrangements for his burial so the planning and execution were left to his bodyguard. Mick Jagger was not able to stay in England for the funeral as he was scheduled to star in the film, Ned Kelly, in Australia. Keith Richards did not attend either.

Marianne had a bit part in the film and accompanied Mick on the long trip trip down under. She went through the motions but was silently upset by Brian's death and everyone's seemingly casual acceptance of it. Her health was below par from anorexia, alcohol abuse and unabated acid trips.

Two days after arriving in Australia, she attempted suicide. She thought she saw Brian's face staring back at her in the hotel mirror, inviting her to join him. She tried jumping out of one of the 14th floor windows but thankfully, they were all sealed shut tight by paint.

She then swallowed 150 Tiunal barbiturates. Marianne was found unresponsive, by Mick and rushed to a convent hospital where she lay in a coma for six days. The last rites were read and her mother was summoned. It was a close call but the nuns took good care of her. She recovered sufficiently to be discharged, and returned to England without Mick to convalesce.

This was not the end of Marianne's dependence on drugs. She continued to flirt with death, and she and others often wondered whether she would wake up each morning. She did not fear death. She thought it would be a welcome relief after spending seemingly countless years here on earth.

Through his death, Brian became the founder member of the 27 Club of the modern era. Jimi Hendrix died in September of the following year. Marianne knew him and performed with him. She claims he tried to seduce her and that she regrets that she had not allowed him to do so.

Janis Joplin died a couple of weeks later of an overdose. She famously said that she made love to thousands of people each night, and then went to bed alone.

Jim Morrisos, poet, lyricist and lead singer of the Doors, died in 1971, on the second anniversary of Brian's death. He was staying in Paris and attempting to get his life back on track after a series of run ins with the law in the USA. However, he still had a penchant for heroin.

The batch he took on the night was too strong for his system, and he died. The heroin was supplied by Marianne's boyfriend at the time, Jean de Breteuil, a handsome, jet setting nobleman who doubled as a drug dealer.

Marianne had had a sense of foreboding about the transaction and stayed home to indulge in her own barbiturates. When the news of Morrison's death broke in the morning, the couple fled to Morocco, to evade being questioned by the authorities.

CHAPTER TWELVE
Alone

Things did not go much better for Mick Jagger either. Towards the end of 1969, during a tour to the USA, the group received criticism that their ticket prices were too high. In a fit of hubris, the Rolling Stones decided that the group were going to stage a free event at the end of the tour. This was intended to rival the Woodstock Festival that had taken place peacefully, in August of that year on the East Coast. Altamont Speedway in the San Francisco Bay Area of Northern California was chosen for the venue.

Due to a late change of venue, the organisers dispensed with any assistance from the authorities. In order to ensure the safety of the generators, they hired the ultimate bad boys, the motorcycle gang, the Hell's Angels. Their payment was to be $500 worth of beer. Gang members were also asked to stay near the front of the stage to prevent anyone interfering with the performers.

The concert featured an impressive line up of Santana; Jefferson Airplane; Crosby, Stills, Nash and Young; the Grateful Dead, and finally the Rolling Stones.

By the time Grateful Dead were scheduled to play, they refused to go on stage because the situation had turned too violent. During the Rolling Stones slot, a fan, in a bright green jumpsuit, who was high on drugs, repeatedly tried to gain access to the stage. When repelled by the Hell's Angels, the enraged man drew a gun and was stabbed to death.

The band had to keep playing else there would have been pandemonium. Other fatalities included an accidental drowning and a hit and run. Several people were injured, cars were stolen and there was a great deal of damage to property.

The incident was featured in 'Gimme Shelter', a film about the Rolling Stones. It appeared to shift responsibility and paint the Hell's Angels in an unfavourable light. There were rumours that they sought revenge in a plot to murder Mick Jagger, but it failed.

In 1970, Marianne decided that their relationship was doomed and decided to leave him. According to her, he did try to pursue her and that the song, 'Wild Horses', that he penned shortly afterwards was an attempt to woo her back.

She took her child and moved back in with her mother which did not work out well. Almost immediately she felt what it was like to lose Mick's protection. Her ex-husband filed for divorce and custody of their son.

Marianne could not escape the hold drugs had her and an acrimonious court battle ensued. Some of her friends were forced, on pain of perjury, to testify that she was an unfit mother.

She was broke, her parents could not afford to keep her, and she tried squatting with friends, to no avail. Ultimately Marianne ended up living on the street. For the next two years she was homeless, sheltered by a bombed out wall in Soho.

Strangers cared for her and her drug habit was sustained by a government sponsored program. She tried to disappear but from time to time she could be found, and friends and family patched her up, ready for her next excursion into obscurity.

After losing almost everything, she found she had a new voice and had grown into the songs that she had sung so glibly as a pretty young starlet. She reclaimed and reframed her image, before relocating to Ireland where she found a faithful following. It took her twenty years to finally free herself from her addictions.

Marianne's singing career traces the evolution of rock through the 70s and 80s. She has shared the stage with a host of famous names and is a seasoned touring artist. She discovered a talent for writing lyrics and poetry and is a published author, who has starred in both films and theatre productions. Several of her works have received critical acclaim and she has been the recipient of some of the industry's most prestigious awards.

Her work can be found on several platforms of the digital age. She has social media accounts and streaming video on demand. Her best performing song has almost twenty million hits. Some of her loyal supporters have followed her since the start of her career but she has gained as many, if not more, ardent fans along the way.

Marianne is still innovating, after six decades in the entertainment industry. Despite several setbacks with her health, she is stronger than ever and looks forward to reaching even greater heights. She knows no limits.

www.ingramcontent.com/pod-product-compliance
Ingram Content Group UK Ltd.
Pitfield, Milton Keynes, MK11 3LW, UK
UKHW021527050225
4457UKWH00039B/703